How To Succeed at Real Estate

When You Don't Really Like People

Amy Fridhi

DEDICATION

This book is dedicated to the hundreds of agents I have crossed paths with.

I have learned something from every single one of you.

Disclaimer: The opinions in this book are entirely my own. Also, I swear sometimes.

CONTENTS

ARE YOU READY?

Are you a real estate agent who is scared to jump into the business? Or have you been at it a few years and don't feel like you're "doing it right"? Maybe you think you can't succeed at real estate because you don't give off used car salesman vibes. Or better yet because you are an introvert, and the thought of spending time with strangers makes you nauseous. Maybe you think you're too short. Or too young. I'm here to tell you to get out of your head and learn a new way to succeed.

I've been in your shoes. I've done the dirty work. I've learned what works (and what doesn't). It's my goal to share it all with you so you can succeed (and enjoy) this wild roller coaster of being a real estate agent.

The first step in succeeding in real estate is finding the

real you. Shut off Selling Sunset and Million Dollar Listing New York. Other than Ryan Serhant (@ryanserhant), that isn't how shit really works (yes, I'm a bit of a fangirl). Take a pause from the Facebook and Instagram posts of all the social media savvy agents out there. This isn't about them; it's about you.

Do you know what you're not going to find in this book? Cold calling scripts. There also won't be any sample "leave behinds" for when you go door-knocking. Why? Because that's not how we roll. If that's what you came here for, please accept my apologies, and request a refund. Or give this book to someone who you think will enjoy it.

What you will find are methods to help you determine how you work best and tips to succeed with your business. There will be personality quizzes and discussions about the soft skills in real estate. I'll also dive into some of the more practical aspects of building a successful real estate business like commissions and brokerages.

I'm going to break down my plan for helping you to

succeed at real estate, and there will be some homework along the way. Throughout the book, I will sprinkle recommended readings, social accounts to follow, and anything else I think will be helpful.

Also, fair warning, I can get a little woo-woo sometimes but trust me, just go with it.

Why me?

You're probably wondering who this crazy pink-haired woman is and what gives her the credibility to teach me how to improve my real estate business. To quote Elyse Myers (of IG and TikTok fame (@elyse_myers), "that's a great question, I'd love to tell you."

I've been in the real estate game personally for over 20 years and professionally for five. I am a licensed Realtor® in Massachusetts and Florida. I love what I do because I have created this life and this way of "doing real estate". I'm also a real estate coach, working with agents like me who are looking to do things differently, and ghostwriter.

Now what's important about the previous two decades of my life is not just the past 5 years as a licensed agent but also the 15 before that. Because, dear reader, I was an educator. I taught all kinds of things from French to web design, from 6th grade to college students. And what I learned most from my time in the classroom is that we are all different, and we all find our own path to success.

There is no one-size-fits-all recipe for real estate success. Some coaches will tell you about their "5-pronged approach" or their "10 lines in the water," and although those are great strategies that work for some, I don't believe they work for everyone. Feel free to disagree but you bought this book, so you must be curious about learning my way of doing things.

Since becoming a real estate agent, I've had the pleasure of working as part of a team, then paired with an amazing partner, and finally as a solo agent. I've had $5 million dollar years and $20 million dollar years (that's total volume btw, if it was commission, I wouldn't need to be writing this book).

I've learned through all those experiences to take what serves me and leave the rest. What worked well for my partner may not work well will cause you to do some soul searching, which will likely benefit not just your business but other aspects of your life too!

CHAPTER 1
Your morning routine, more than just coffee

What would a real estate agent book be if it didn't begin by talking about your morning routine? All (and I mean all) the business gurus and entrepreneur experts out there will tell you what you should and shouldn't do with your morning routine. And to be honest, I agree with a lot of it.

Does it need to start at 5am? Heck no. Should it start before noon? Probably. The important part is that you find what works for you. Have kids at home? I recommend doing your best to at least find an hour of quiet before they jump out of bed. Have cats? Use their 6am request for breakfast as a nudge to start your day. Whenever you decide to begin your morning, try to be consistent with when and what you do.

For me a perfect morning consists of 3 things: mindfulness, coffee, and cats. Do I wish it included more exercise? You betcha. But right now, this is what it looks like.

I meditate. A lot. Like a lot lot. Some days my husband is concerned that I'm turning into a monk. It's what works for me. Then I drink coffee and talk to my cats. It's what calms me and clears my mind for the day ahead.

Ask yourself: what helps me to find some quiet space in my mind?

For some that's prayer, for others it's a walk in the woods. For me it's sitting cross legged on the floor with incense burning. Find what yours is and make it the first thing you do in the morning (after brushing your teeth).

As a real estate agent, it can be difficult to set and keep boundaries. I encourage you to set one in the morning of not reading (or worse answering) any work-related emails, texts, or calls. Use this morning time to find your Zen so you can spend the rest of the day kicking ass.

If you're curious about meditation, there are plenty of apps out there like Calm and InsightTimer. I personally use my Peloton app (find me there @amyFreeDee).

Looking for a great book about meditation? Check out: **Real Happiness: The Power of Meditation**.

If you are an overachiever and want a more robust morning routine, I encourage you to check out Hal Elrod's Miracle Morning for Real Estate Agents. He's got a great mnemonic device to remind you of the six parts of a great morning: silence, affirmations, visualizations, exercise, reading, and scribing (SAVERS). I really like Hal's method and have done it from time to time. Maybe this is a sign I should get back into it.

The important lesson here is that your morning routine needs to fit your life, your schedule, and your rhythm. It's ok if you try one kind of routine and it doesn't quite work for you. Just keep tweaking until it does. This is *your* morning routine. Not mine, not the agent down the street, and not your Broker's.

You will start to notice that consistency with your morning routine helps you to be more patient with clients and more balanced throughout the day. I can almost guarantee that if I miss my morning hippie session, my day will go off the rails at some point. Consistency is key my friends.

#morningroutine

CHAPTER 2
Don't try to be somebody else

When I first got licensed and had no idea what the heck I was doing, I did what had always helped me in life, I watched, and I imitated. I watched all the agents on my team. I watched other agents in my office and at open houses. I took the parts that I thought made them successful and tried to implement them so that I too could be successful. Now, this was only partially helpful.

Watching some of the luxury agents in Boston was awesome, and gave me #goals, but I also realized it's not who I am. Am I smart enough to work in luxury real estate? Of course. Will I feel true to myself while doing it if I carry a Chanel bag and talk about the country club? Not so much. I had to find what worked for me.

The same thing happened when I watched outgoing agents who talked non-stop while touring their clients at an open house. That may be what attracted their client to them and that's great. But that's not my style, and as a result, those aren't my clients.

Similarly, some agents that I saw were super social,

chatting up a room full of people without breaking a sweat. Not my jam. In fact, the thought of chatting up a room full of people makes me sweat. But again, if that's what works for you, I want you to go with it.

Making the move from education to real estate resulted in some soul searching of the best kind. I had a chance to create the persona I wanted the world to see. I thought long and hard about what made me who I am, what was important to me, and how I wanted to be perceived by others.

Ask yourself: what 3 words would my friends use to describe me?

I've come to decide that I am, above all, authentic. Aside from my pink hair, what you see is what you get. I will always be my authentic self when meeting clients, other agents, or writing this book. Trying to be someone or something you are not is exhausting. This work is already hard, we don't need to make it harder.

Once you figure out the three (or more) words that really describe you, think about how you will share that information with the world. Unlikely you're going to rent a billboard and plaster them up there, but maybe you infuse them into your social media posts or mention them when you meet clients for the first time. The more you use these words daily, the more they will become a clear and present part of who you are. Don't underestimate the power of putting those words into the universe.

This same concept carries through to what you wear and what you drive. As real estate agents, we feel the need to have a certain "look" and to be perceived as successful, whether that's based on our actual track record or the car we drive. Don't ask me why as an industry we have gotten so caught up in this, but we have, so let's use it to our advantage.

Are there agents that wear mini-skirts and stilettos? Yes (mostly in Miami). Is that what I will be wearing? Hell to the no. It's not who I am. I choose to wear clothes that present the best version of me. Part of this (for all agents) is knowing the colors that work for you and the styles that flatter. But also, what makes you, you. I am known for a great statement necklace, and 99% of the time I will have one on. I know agents who are famous for their sneaker collection or their neckties.

There is no right or wrong, there is only what is right for you.

True story, I once wore really high designer platform wedges to an open house because I thought it would help me fit in with the wealthy crowd who was likely to be there. Well, I almost tumbled down the back steps a few times and I think the blisters are still healing.

#beyou

CHAPTER 3
The nuts and bolts of where you work

If you're a newly licensed agent, chances are your mailboxes (virtual and actual) are filling up with recruiting letters and offers of high commission, no desk fees, and a laundry list of other benefits. If you're a veteran agent who had a good year, you're probably also getting calls from other brokerages trying to sway you to come work with them. Either way this chapter will be helpful for you now as you embark on this journey or down the road when you are ready for a change.

In the spirit of transparency, I have worked for three different brokerages. I currently still work for two of them (don't forget, I'm licensed in two states). Let me explain. When I first got licensed, I was so wowed by the fact that someone wanted me to come to work with them that I basically jumped at the first opportunity that I got. It wasn't a bad choice by any means; I just didn't put much thought into it (nor did I do all the homework and question asking I'm encouraging you to do).

In hindsight, I gave up a LOT of my commission income that first year. I was at a 50/50 split. I did get a lot of benefits and I was part of a team that was an incredible learning experience for me. It was a great start and taught me a lot about the business.

I'm about to breakdown a process for you to handle all these flattering calls and emails and really drill down to what's important and ultimately what will help you succeed. Let's talk through the things you should be thinking about and questions you should be asking when trying to determine which brokerage or company to join.

First thing is first. Remember, they need you as much as you need them, so you are in the driver's seat. Don't let any high-pressure sales tactics or relentless phone calls get to you. Keep saying no until all your questions are answered and you are satisfied with what you're offered.

Here are the six main categories of things you should consider when choosing what brokerage to join.

Money stuff

Let's be honest, this is the reason (or at least one of the reasons) many of us decide to transition into a career in real estate. Unlimited earning potential. The harder you work, the more money you make (at least, that's what they want you to think). Many non-agents look at the sale price of a house, do some quick math and immediately say "Holy shit! These Realtors® make a lot of money for not doing much work!"

What they don't know is the many hands in the pot, all asking for a piece of that commission. Let's talk about that now.

Commission Split. You will hear lots of numbers thrown out about this. Everything from 50/50 to 90/10 to even "100%!! Keep all your commission!!" Remember what you've always been told, if it sounds too good to be true, it probably is. Many commission splits operate like rungs on a ladder in that the higher you get in the business (your total volume sold), the better your split (more money in your pocket).

In discussing the split with potential brokerages, be sure to understand what you get in exchange for their piece of the pie. The 10%, 20%, or 50% portion of your commission should be directly correlated to the number of perks you get for working with that brokerage. For example, if you've got a place with 100% commission (meaning they take nothing from you), expect nothing in return. You will be paying for all your own marketing materials, a CRM, a desk, and probably even photocopies.

For some people, this 100% commission model works. I'm not one of them.

Other models have a more gracious split, let's say they take 30% of your commission but in exchange you get an assigned desk in the office, they have a transaction manager to help you with all the paperwork we do, you get free copies (these add up) and even done-for-you marketing. In my world, these are all time savers and, more importantly, things I'm not good at. I will gladly pay someone else to do my marketing if it means I can spend more time working on building relationships.

Ask yourself: is my time best used doing a bunch of things I'm not really good at?

Cap. For companies that do have a commission split (non-100% brokerages), many also have something called a cap. This means that after you have done a certain amount of transaction volume (ex. sold $10M worth of homes) or given them a certain amount of commission (ex. $20,000), you no longer have to split your commissions with them. Be sure to ask about this and do the math to see what that trajectory would look like for you.

Desk fee and/or other fees. You may come across a brokerage that requires a desk fee in addition to, or in place of a commission split. The amount of these varies. Sometimes it means an actual desk, other times it just means use of the office and its supplies. What I'm about to say next may sound crazy but ask about supplies. Do you pay for stationery? What about yard signs? Business cards? These expenses add up and are an additional task for you to sort out. Some people find it worth it to handle these on their own. Others prefer it be absorbed into the "desk fee" and taken care of for them.

There is no right or wrong answer when it comes to which compensation model to choose. It is ultimately up to you in terms of the system and structure that you think will work best for your situation, motivation, and knowledge.

Corporate vs independent vs virtual (yes, that's a thing)

You've likely heard of many of the corporate companies; these are brokerages like Coldwell Banker, Century 21, Berkshire Hathaway, and Keller Williams. These brokerages have offices in cities and states across the country, all overseen by a broker/manager. These larger name brokerages tend to have much larger agent rosters as well as more administrative staff. There are also smaller, independent brokerages, which are the more local offices. They have fewer agents under their umbrella and usually only 1 or 2 staff members. These are usually named something connected to the area. In Florida we have Royal Shell Realty and in Boston there is Boston City Properties. You get the drift.

Keep in mind that each of these first two brokerages have brick and mortar locations, however, there is little to no requirement that you go to the office. As I'm sure you've learned by now, most of your work will be done from your phone, laptop, and car. The nice thing about a brick-and-mortar office is that you have somewhere to go if you prefer working in an office type setting. It's also a great way to network and learn from others.

More of a digital nomad? There's a brokerage for that too. One company that has really embraced this model is eXp. Beware, there are agents who have very strong opinions on this brokerage. I am neutral, like Switzerland. eXp is built on a virtual model where all trainings, meetings, and mentoring happen in their online platform. They do not have a physical presence, although I do know some eXp agents who rent office space for their teams for co-working and meetings.

What it comes down to is personal preference. Which type of work environment suits you best? Do you like large groups or prefer smaller settings? Which type of workplace do you think would be more conducive to your success?

Culture

Last, but certainly not least, do you feel comfortable in the culture of the office? This is super important for us introverted types. If you value quiet and appreciate boundaries, make sure you're not walking into an office that feels more like a frat party. Do you love volunteering and want to ensure it is valued in your office? Make sure you look for that. You'll know a good culture fit when you find it.

How long do I have to stay?

I don't want you thinking about jumping ship before you even get on board, but I also want you to know that if you join a brokerage and after a few months you realize it is most definitely not the right place for you, it's ok to change. Real estate agents are independent contractors; we get to choose where to hang our licenses. No one is recommending changing brokerages like a round of speed dating, but moving to one that better aligns with your goals and values is totally acceptable.

#findtherightfit

CHAPTER 4

Find your tribe (aka your ideal clients)

I know, I know. I sound like one of those Millennial life coaches (no offense). But seriously, to be successful and for it to feel easy, it's important to find clients who "fit" with you. Can I help just about anyone sell their home? More than likely. Am I going to enjoy the experience if the seller is a control freak and is constantly bossing me around? Probably not. That's not my client.

Some real estate coaches and gurus will have you create your ideal client avatar (ICA), and I don't necessarily think this is a bad idea. Thinking about who you want to work with puts it out into the universe, making it more likely that those people will find you.

I am not a social butterfly. But I am an expert at building relationships (more on that later). I know what exhausts me, so I don't do it. Networking event on Thursday? No thanks. Coffee with a referral partner? Sign me up.

Think about the people you choose to be friends with. The people who you don't mind getting texts from beginning early in the morning and again late at night.

These are the people who will make great clients. As an introvert, or someone who is otherwise exhausted being around people, it's important that you work with people who don't drain your energy (you know who they are).

Your ideal client may not be who you think it is. It's important to think beyond the neighborhood and price point and really drill down to who they are and what they do. Are you a parent? Do you like being around other parents? This may influence who your ideal client is.

Ask yourself: what type of people am I most drawn to?

Are you a veteran and find commonalities with others who have served their country? This population may be a good place to look for your ideal client. Really homing in on your ICA takes some time, but always try to be thoughtful about the clients you are working with, which you really enjoy, and which you might not choose to work with again. This does not make them bad people; it just means that they are someone else's ideal client.

There are two main reasons that you want to identify your ideal client early. The first is that it will help you narrow down your marketing. There is an old saying "if you're marketing to everyone, you're marketing to no one." If you know that your ideal client is a millennial with a dog and a master's degree, this will direct your social media strategy, what referral partners you choose, and even how you show up to a listing appointment.

The second reason is that working with your ideal client will be an incredibly rewarding and energizing experience for you. When you begin to feel synergies with your clients and build strong relationships, it makes work much more enjoyable, and you get that much better faster.

#findyourtribe

CHAPTER 5
The alphabet of things

OK, this one is a doozy, and it's likely (actually, guaranteed) that I won't cover everything here. But I will do my best. Working in real estate requires a figurative and literal toolbox. This list will hopefully help you to start filling up those toolboxes.

**By the way, these will be in alphabetical order, not order of importance.*

Accountability. You need to hold yourself accountable to do what you say you are going to do. Unlike a traditional workplace where your boss gives you deadlines and your paycheck depends on you meeting them, there is no boss here. You are the boss. You need to give yourself deadlines. That may look like setting yourself an assignment to call a certain number of clients each week, or to attend a training on a new topic once a month. Whatever those things are is up to you, but it's also up to you to make sure you do them.

Bestie. You need a work bestie. Real estate can be a wacky business and finding someone who "gets it" and who you can vent to or problem-solve with is

HUGE! This could be another new agent, could be a colleague, or a coach. What's important is that it's someone you can be vulnerable with and who understands the nuances of the business we are in.

Calculator. You will do lots of math. From calculating down payments to calculating your commission. You don't want to do this stuff in your head. Get a calculator.

Disinfectant. Spray, wipes, whatever. In your trunk. You will touch a lot of doorknobs and light switches. You will also shake a lot of hands. That's a lot of germs. I've even had a kid wipe his chocolate covered hands on a white couch during an open house. Make sure you've got cleaning supplies.

Energy. Being a Realtor® comes with long hours and some sleepless nights. It's crucial to know when you need to take it easy so you have energy for upcoming tasks. I am an introvert, so I take it easy on Friday when I know I have an open house on a Saturday. I will need every ounce of energy I have for that open house. It is MORE THAN OK to respect your energy and your limits.

Finances. As an independent contractor, you can now deduct business expenses. And they will add up faster than you expect. From MLS dues to gas mileage to closing gifts. You will want to ensure you track these numbers and keep your finances in order. It makes life a lot easier during tax time.

Google. Real estate school may have taught you how many square feet in an acre (34,560), but you'll need to know a lot more than that. The Google will help you find the assessor's database in the city/town your clients are looking. It will also help you to understand what a Title V is (a very crappy topic, stay far away if you can). Want to know how far a property is from the local elementary school, Google maps has the answer. Want to see what the surrounding land looks like, hit up Google Earth.

Humor. Things don't always go as planned. And sometimes you're showing a house with a dead bird in the bedroom (true story). It's helpful to keep a sense of humor about things. I don't mean that you should make constant jokes and act like a clown, more so just keep things light and low stress.

Inspector. A good inspector is hard to find. Ask around, get recommendations, and once you get one, guard them like a treasure. In my opinion, buyers must be knowledgeable about what is likely the largest purchase they have ever made. To do that, you need an expert to go through the home and look at things that the rest of us know very little about (heating systems, roof shingles, plumbing, etc.)

Join. Join networking groups, community organizations, PTOs, or any place that is going to help you to meet more people. Now I know this book is for those of us who don't particularly like people. That's why we need to choose our people carefully. Don't just join any old thing. Pick it like you would pick a friend.

Koffee. Sorry, I already used the letter C. If you already drink coffee, you'll be drinking more. If you don't, you'll start. It's a great way to meet clients for the first time, it helps get you going for those early morning weekend inspections, and it's just all around good for business.

Laptop. You can't bring your big bulky desktop from 2002 in the car. Get yourself something that travels. I once wrote an offer in a McDonald's parking lot (their Wi-Fi is surprisingly reliable). If you think you're going on vacation and not doing any work, think again. You'll need to bring a laptop.

Measuring tape. You will always have clients ask if their couch will fit in the living room or if the backyard is big enough for a pool. Save the day with a measuring tape.

No. Know when to say no. It is easy to fall into the trap of wanting to keep every deal and every client because that's what pays your bills. But sometimes, it's ok to say no if it is someone or something that is just zapping your energy. It is also ok to say no to absurd requests. Your clients work with you to buy/sell real estate. Walking their dog or picking up their dry-cleaning is not your job. Maintaining healthy boundaries will ensure that you are in this for the long haul.

Optimism. This career can beat you down. It can be rough to get traction. It's important to keep a positive attitude and stay optimistic that you are going to be successful, because you will. Putting positive vibes out into the universe helps to ensure that good stuff returns to you. Trust me on this one.

Phone. A smartphone preferably. I know you're laughing right now but there are still agents running around out there with flip phones and they will make your life difficult. As an agent you are on the go and working from the road—a lot. Having a smartphone that can access email, MLS, and call a client is critical.

Quiet. Know when to be quiet. Know when to listen, whether to an upset seller, an annoyed agent, or a disappointed buyer. Sometimes they don't want answers; they just want to feel heard. Give them that space.

Realtor® Designation. Hopefully you've learned the difference between a Realtor® and real estate agent. All Realtors® are real estate agents, but not all real estate agents are Realtors®. I know, it sounds like some sort of brain teaser. Realtors® have taken an additional level of training and are bound to a code of ethics. As a Realtor® you will have the opportunity to join boards at the local, state, and national levels, as well as to attend conferences and earn additional designations and certifications.

Sensible shoes. I know a lot of you ladies probably love your high heels but believe me when I tell you to keep a spare pair of shoes in your trunk. It's not unusual to show a property to a client in the rain and the backyard is a giant mud puddle. Or you just do too much walking, and your feet hurt. You'll be thankful you've got something clean and comfy stashed in the car.

Tracker. Tracking clients is crucial. You want to have all their important information (name, address, phone) as well as highlights (birthdays, dog's name) saved in an organized way. It's also helpful to track their budget, properties they have viewed, etc. This can be done on paper (not ideal), in a spreadsheet (better), or in a customer relationship management tool (best). Oftentimes your broker will provide access to one, but there are also CRMs that you can purchase and use on your own.

Umbrella. It will rain when you have showings. Unless you live in the desert. And even there it might.

Volunteer. This is a great way to meet people who have a common interest. Volunteer for a cause that matters to you. Doesn't hurt if it is Instagram worthy. I'm thinking of things like helping to build a house for Habitat for Humanity or walking dogs at the local animal shelter. Volunteering is also just good for the soul.

Welcoming attitude. First impressions matter whether you are on floor duty, working an open house, or meeting new clients. If you greet everyone you come across with a smile and a welcoming attitude, they are more likely to stick around to interact with you and hopefully become clients.

X. Seriously, you thought I would come up with something that started with X?? (If you have one, please send it to amy@amyfridhi.com)

Yellow pages. Just kidding, no one uses those anymore, I just couldn't think of anything that started with Y.

Zillow. I know, I'm going to catch a lot of heat for this one. But here is the deal, our clients are looking here. We need to know what they are seeing. Sellers look here to figure out what they think their home is worth. You want to know that number before you go on a listing appointment so that you can set their expectations and explain why that number may not be the most accurate. And if I'm being totally honest, it's often a lot easier to find basic property specs on the Zillow app than it is to log into MLS and search there.

#fromAtoZ

CHAPTER 6
This isn't Match.com

Ok, true story, I met my husband on Match.com. But that is not where you are going to meet clients and build lasting relationships. (Unless you are one of my agent friends who has been successful in doing this, you know who you are.)

I am not saying this to brag, but I literally have a PhD in relationship building. No, I'm not some sort of dating expert, but I am an expert in building successful educational partnerships. I have used my research and experience in this area and translated it to the real estate world.

If you listen to enough coaches, brokers, and experienced agents, you're sure to hear the phrase "know, like, trust." This explains the process a person goes through when building a relationship with you. To take it a level deeper, the three factors that go into this are authenticity, logic, and empathy.

This may sound complicated and exhausting, but it doesn't have to be.

Ask yourself: what characteristics make someone likeable?

Relationships matter. Not just the relationships with your clients, but also with your colleagues, and other agents in the business. Let's break this down into three parts.

Clients

At the end of the day, you get paid if your clients are successful in buying or selling a home. These are the primary people in your relationship pyramid. You are their primary support. They must trust you, appreciate you, and value you. This is all earned, not given. Building this trust and appreciation can be done with a few simple steps. First, communicate. I don't mean to stalk them on Facebook and text them constantly. What I mean is to stay in communication with them. Make sure they know that you are available to them. Set clear expectations about your working hours and response time (we all need more balance in this area). If they call or text with a question, don't leave them hanging for days. If they request a floor plan or property photos, send it to them. These sound like basic things, but you would be surprised how many agents don't do this. Second, share information. Sometimes we feel like we are protecting our clients by not telling them what a nightmare the seller of their dream home is. I'm not encouraging you to go into every gory detail, but make sure they understand the challenges, while at the same time, ensuring that you are taking care of business.

Third, show your appreciation. Remember, this is a referral business. If a client feels appreciated by you, they will likely want their friends to feel the same thing and will pass along your business card when the opportunity arises. If you appreciate your clients, they will appreciate you. This can be as simple as sending a birthday card or gift for a new baby, and as elaborate as hosting a housewarming party for them after closing. There is no right or wrong. It all depends on your comfort level (and budget). Doing these three things will build solid, long-lasting relationships with your clients that will reward you for years to come.

Colleagues

In this book, I use colleagues to mean other agents in your office. You are probably thinking, "I'm an independent contractor why would I need to build relationships with my colleagues? They are my competition!" Trust me on this one. One great way to get experience and learn the ropes is by shadowing more experienced agents. To do this, you need to make friends with those in your office and show them that you are interested in learning.

Many more experienced agents also don't host their own open houses but have promised their sellers that there would be one, so the best option for them is to have another agent host it. Believe me when I tell you that hosting an open house can be an amazing way to practice being an agent and to get leads. You get practice being an agent because you welcome people to the property, describe the home's features, and answer questions. Practice makes perfect. It is also a great way to get clients. In this day an age of online property listings (think Realtor.com and Zillow), lots of would-be homebuyers find a place they want to see online and decide to go to the open house on their own. If you are personable, knowledgeable, and make the ask, it is highly likely these would-be buyers become your clients. As a first-year agent I had a shockingly high conversion rate at open houses. Meeting someone in person is different (and better) than seeing their headshot and reading their bio online. All this to say, making friends with colleagues opens the door for you to open actual doors for new clients.

Another reason you want to be buddies is to get the inside scoop on new listings. Often agents share information among themselves before a listing goes live in MLS. This is helpful if there is a shortage of inventory as well as if you have a client looking for a very specific size/type/location of home.

The last reason you want to make yourself known among the colleagues in your office is for referrals. You may all work in an office in Chicago, but some agents may only focus on specific neighborhoods, whereas you focus on others. If an agent gets a lead who is looking in a neighborhood they don't service, but they know that you do, they will likely refer this client to you (for a referral fee). Experienced colleagues can also be a wealth of information. If you are lucky enough to get a listing as a new agent, pricing may be a challenge. There is no shame in bringing in a more experienced agent from your office to look at the home and help you determine a price for the property.

Too many agents operate with a scarcity mindset and come across as competitive and not super cooperative. I am hoping to see a shift in this soon. The truth is, there is plenty to go around, and the more we support each other, the more we all succeed.

Other agents in the industry

Some of the things I outlined above for your colleagues holds true for agents from other offices too. But the real reason you want to network with those outside of your brokerage is so that they know you, like you, and learn to trust you. Where have we heard that before?

This comes in incredibly handy when you submit an offer in a competitive market. Rather than just being a name listed on the top of an offer or contract, you are the agent they saw at their open house last weekend or who said nice things about their new listing on Facebook. When working with sellers, I explain that one of the factors affecting the strength of an offer we receive is the agent who wrote it. If I know that the agent is trustworthy and responsive, I know that there is a better likelihood that the transaction successfully closes. Conversely, if the agent is someone that I've never heard of or who is a real wildcard, I may have some reservations about accepting the offer, even if it is all cash and over asking. Trust me.

Another somewhat unknown reason to network with agents outside your office is that you don't know what opportunities exist for you. When I was a new agent, I was working with some buyers and every time I brought them to see properties in a particular neighborhood, it was the same listing agent. I was like "shit, she's doing something right." She was always incredibly kind to me and so knowledgeable about the properties. I went home and thought "I want to be like her." So, I called her up and asked her to coffee. We had coffee and lunch a handful of times and then she said, "why don't you come join me and we can work together?" It was like opening a gift on Christmas. Not only did I double my sales volume that year, but I learned so much from her and gained valuable experience and exposure. I am forever grateful. All because I decided to build a relationship with an agent outside of my office. See, you never know.

BONUS: Your friends and family

Don't forget to try to keep some sort of life balance. Spend time with friends and family, find some downtime to recharge and connect.

Whether it's clients, colleagues, or industry peers, your reputation is important. No matter how big you think your market is, believe me when I tell you that news travels. It is important to have integrity in your transactions and respect for your peers and colleagues. The rewards you will get from that are something that money cannot buy.

Remember the Golden Rule: Do unto others as you would have them do unto you.

#relationshipsmatter

CHAPTER 7
I'm an introvert, how about you?

My name is Amy, and I am an introvert.

If you know me well, you know this to be true, even though I am fun to be around and am good at building relationships. However, my introvertedness affects how I do business, so I plan for it. That's the goal of this chapter. To help you identify your personality strengths and use them to up-level your real estate biz.

There is no one-size-fits-all Realtor®. There, I said it. Just as there are all kinds of people in this world, there are all kinds of people in the real estate world. There is no one right "type" of personality that guarantees success in this business. There is a good chance you have a different personality type than I do, and different than the person who sat next to you during your real estate licensing course. And that's more than ok, because as my grandma used to say, "There's a lid for every pot." My type of clients may not be your type. And the type drawn to you may think I'm batshit crazy. What's important is that you figure out your personality strengths and use them to focus your business.

Ask yourself: what do I think I know about my personality?

You've probably all seen personality tests online. I don't mean the kind on Buzzfeed like "What kind of cocktail are you?" or "Which Disney character are you most like?" I mean the kind that drills down to your fundamental traits. I'll highlight a few and provide links to them online so you can take the quizzes and learn about your strengths if you don't already know.

Myers-Briggs

Officially known as the Myers-Briggs Type Indicator (MBTI), this personality test helps people see that some of the "random" behaviors they exhibit are consistent and can be used to identify their personality strengths.

The characteristics are divided into eight basic categories: extraversion (E), sensing (S), thinking (T), judgment (J), introversion (I), intuition (N), feeling (F), and perception (P). Each personality type is made up of four of these.

Some of the concepts are easy to grasp, such as introvert vs. extrovert or thinking vs. feeling. Just hearing those words, you can probably already guess which fits you best. There are plenty of (unofficial) places to take free tests online; one of the best is Truity[1]. If you take the test and share your results on social media, be sure to tag me @amy_fridhi!

Knowing your personality type will help you to organize your workday better, develop skills to deal with clients, and focus on ways of building your business that leverage your strengths.

For those of you wondering, I am an ISTJ.

Here is a chart that shows the various combinations that make up a person's MBTI.

INTJ THE ARCHITECT imaginative strategic planners	INTP THE LOGICIAN innovative curious logical	ENTJ THE COMMANDER bold imaginative strong-willed	ENTP THE DEBATER smart curious intellectual
INFJ THE ADVOCATE quiet mystical idealist	INFP THE MEDIATOR poetic kind altruistic	ENFJ THE PROTAGONIST charismatic inspiring natural leaders	ENFP THE CAMPAIGNER enthusiastic creative sociable
ISTJ THE LOGISTICIAN practical fact-minded reliable	ISFJ THE DEFENDER protective warm caring	ESTJ THE EXECUTIVE organized punctual leader	ESFJ THE CONSUL caring social popular
ISTP THE VIRTUOSO bold practical experimental	ISFP THE ADVENTURER artistic charming explorers	ESTP THE ENTREPRENEUR smart strategic planners	ESFP THE ARCHITECT imaginative strategic planners

Enneagram

The Enneagram is relatively new on the scene, at least for me, although I suspect personality gurus have been using it for years. There are nine enneagram "types," which provide a summary of your personality. The Enneagram helps you to see yourself at a deeper and more objective level.

In other words, it helps you to figure yourself out.

Unlike the Myers-Briggs, which just has a jumble of letters, the Enneagram has delightful labels for each type. These include the reformer, the helper, the achiever, the individualist, the investigator, the loyalist, the enthusiast, the challenger, and the peacemaker.

As you can probably guess, the labels given for each type summarize the characteristics of that person. For example, the helper is caring, generous, people-pleasing, etc. In comparison, the enthusiast is spontaneous and sometimes scattered. There is no right or wrong enneagram type when it comes to being in the real estate business. What is important is that you understand your type.

I recommend taking an online test to learn what your enneagram type is. Again, Truity leads the pack with the easiest free version of the test[2].

Once you know your type, you will likely find all kinds of fun and interesting posts on social media about the Enneagram.

Here is a chart outlining the nine enneagram types[3].

Type One The Reformer	Principled, purposeful, self-controlled & perfectionistic Dislike sloppiness and error, attracted to order and high standards for self and others
Type Two The Helper	Caring, generous, people-pleasing & intrusive Dislike solitude and impersonal dealings, attracted to service and making personal connections
Type Three The Achiever	Adaptable, self-developing, efficient & image-conscious Dislike ineffectiveness and lack of ambition, attracted to success and recognition
Type Four The Individualist	Intuitive, expressive, individualistic & temperamental Dislike uniformity and regulation, attracted to creativity and putting their personal mark on things
Type Five The Investigator	Perceptive, innovative, secretive & detached Dislike intrusions on their time and space, attracted to depth and learning
Type Six The Loyalist	Committed, responsible, anxious & suspicious Dislike unpredictability and rapid change, attracted to clear structures and foresight
Type Seven The Enthusiast	Spontaneous, versatile, talkative & scattered Dislike limitations and routines, attracted to new possibilities and excitement
Type Eight The Challenger	Self-confident, decisive, willful & confrontational Dislike indecisiveness and indirectness, attracted to strength and strategic action
Type Nine Peacemakers	Calm, reassuring, agreeable & complacent Dislike tension and conflict, attracted to harmony and stability

Type A vs. Type B

We have all heard people refer to themselves as "type A" personalities (maybe even you), meaning they are organized and prefer structure over chaos. They often have very neat desks and perfect handwriting.

Our "type B" friends, on the other hand, are much more laid back and less "tightly wound." This doesn't make them any less successful; it's just a part of who they are and how they function in the world. This quick test[4] will help you to confirm your type.

There are, of course, many other types of personality tests, all of which contribute to you learning about yourself, your skills, and your strengths. Careful not to use these to put yourself in a corner (ex., I'm an introvert, so I can't network.), but rather to leverage your strengths (ex., I'm an introvert, which makes me an amazing listener).

How does this help you?

Let's review some personality traits and how they could help you in real estate.

Enneagram type 2: The helper. You are a people pleaser, which means your clients will LOVE you. You are attracted to making personal connections. That's what this business is all about!!

Enneagram type 8: The Challenger. You are direct and confrontational. This will benefit you in a challenging negotiation or with clients who take advantage of your time.

Myers-Briggs ESTJ (Extraverted, Observant, Thinking, and Judging personality traits.) You have a calm, stable demeanor. You also have the values of honesty and dedication, two things your clients will be fortunate to have with you as their agent.

Myers-Briggs INFP (Introverted, Intuitive, Feeling, and Prospecting personality traits.) You are quieter, but also a good listener; clients value this. You can understand how they feel about a property before they even say something.

Homework

Take some time to do one or more of these personality tests to learn about yourself and what strengths you have that you may not even realize.

#introvertsunite

CHAPTER 8
My money don't jiggle jiggle

Time to get your calculator, we are about to do a lot of math. But it's important math. We are talking about how much money you're going to make.

Commission.

Let's start at the top. This math is the same whether you represent the buyer or the seller. Let's assume a property is listed in MLS as 6% commission. Let's also assume the property is listed at $1,000,000. The total commission that the sellers of that property will be paying to the agents of the transaction is $60,000.

$1,000,000 x 0.6 = $60,000

Now let's assume that the listing agent is a fair and equitable human being and is splitting the commission 50/50, paying 3% to herself and 3% to the buyer's agent. That means each side will get a gross commission (GCI) of $30,000. We can calculate this in two ways:

$1,000,000 x 0.3 = $30,000

OR $60,000/2 = $30,000

Most brokerages take a percentage off the top (before any split), typically between 4-6%, so in this case, let's say 5% goes to the brokerage. That means of the \$30,000 GCI, \$1,500 will go to the brokerage. That leaves you with <u>\$28,500</u>.

\$30,000 x .05 = \$1,500

\$30,000 - \$1,500 = \$28,500

Splits

In this example, we will pretend you are a solo agent, and because you are new, your split with your brokerage is 60/40. 60% goes to you, and 40% goes to them. In this case, you would get \$17,100, and they would get \$11,400.

\$28,500 x .06 = \$17,100

And \$28,500 x .04 = \$11,400

Taxes

As an independent contractor, you need to pay your own taxes. Please make sure you do this quarterly; otherwise, you will be very sad in April when income tax filing is due. This number varies widely based on your household income, dependents, etc. (I am neither an accountant nor CPA, please consult a professional.) For this example, let's say you are in the 30% tax bracket, which means 30% of your income goes to taxes. Taking the number from above of $17,100, you would pay $5,130 in taxes, and you would get to keep $11,970.

$17,100 x .3 = $5,130 (amount you pay to taxes)

And

$17,100 - $5,130 = $11,970 (commission you keep)

So, in summary, based on the example above, from a Gross Commission Income (GCI) of $30,000, you will get to keep $11,970. These numbers vary with splits and tax brackets (among other things), but this should help to give you some perspective.

Ask yourself: am I ready to pay my own taxes?

Commission Ladders

A commission ladder is a chart that most brokerages

use to determine payment for their agents. These are often negotiable. The more experienced you are, or the more volume you sold in a previous year, likely results in higher placement on the ladder. As a new agent, you often start at the lowest step on the ladder.

Like an actual ladder, you climb the commission ladder as you grow. This matters for two reasons. First, you want the best initial placement on the ladder. If you start at the lowest rung, you have more rungs to reach the top. If you can negotiate to start one higher, that's one step closer to the top. Also, by keeping an eye on the ladder, you can understand how much volume (total sales) you need to reach the next step. Make sense?

Let's look at an example of a commission ladder and do some calculations to understand better what ends up in your pocket. To keep things simple (and to manifest big money), let's stick with the $1,000,000 property price.

$1,000,000 property, 6% commission		
Total Commission=		$60,000
Your Share (3%)=		$30,000
Split	**You**	**Broker**
50/50	$15,000	$15,000
60/40	$18,000	$12,000
70/30	$21,000	$9,000
80/20	$24,000	$6,000
90/10	$27,000	$3,000
100/0	$30,000	$0

Don't forget, you still need to pay taxes out of this.

Curious about what the numbers look like at lower price points? Here are two examples of the commission ladder using a $500,000 sale and a $250,000 sale:

$500,000 property, 6% commission		
Total Commission=		$30,000
Your Share (3%)=		$15,000
Split	**You**	**Broker**
50/50	$7,500	$7,500
60/40	$9,000	$6,000
70/30	$10,500	$4,500
80/20	$12,000	$3,000
90/10	$13,500	$1,500
100/0	$15,000	$0

$250,000 property, 6% commission		
	Total Commission=	$15,000
	Your Share (3%)=	$7,500
Split	**You**	**Broker**
50/50	$3,750	$3,750
60/40	$4,500	$3,000
70/30	$5,250	$2,250
80/20	$6,000	$1,500
90/10	$6,750	$750
100/0	$7,500	$0

Cap

You will hear some brokerages discuss a "cap." This means that after you have paid a certain amount of commission, you don't split with them anymore. Basically, you reach the 100/0 rung of the ladder. This "cap" amount varies, but it is worth asking when you are interviewing brokerages.

Other types of models – Transaction Fee

In addition to this traditional model of the commission ladder and cap, some brokerages will offer you to hang your license with them for a certain fee per sale. The amount of the fee and what it includes can vary widely. There may also be a "desk fee" that you pay no matter what and a "transaction fee" that you pay each time you have an actual transaction.

When exploring this model with a brokerage, be aware that you will need to pay for many things on your own. This includes everything from marketing, E&O insurance, and even photocopies. Here is a list of potential expenses you may have to handle if you work for a transaction fee-based brokerage (reshared from The Close[5].)

Agent Transaction Fee - Transaction fee charged to the agent at closing - $100-$250

Buyer Transaction Fee - Transaction fee charged to the buyer at closing - $200-$350

Listing Transaction Fee - Transaction fee charged to the seller at closing - $200-$350

Personal Transaction Fee - Fee for agents on personal transactions -$300-$500

Franchise Fee - Fee paid by agent to the franchisor - 5-8% of GCI

Desk Fee - Fee for a reserved desk or area in the office - $50-$150

Office Fee - Fee for a private or shared office (includes desk) - $200-$1,000

Brokerage Advertising Fee - Monthly fee paid to support marketing the brokerage - $25/month

Setup Fees - includes business cards, website setup, etc) - $150-$300

Errors and Omissions Insurance Fees - Fee paid to cover the cost of the E&O - $25-$60/month

Transaction Coordination - Contract-to-closing file management - $300-$600/transaction

Showing Service Fee - Fee charged monthly or per listing - $20/month or $75/listing

Signs and Lockboxes - Sign rental/installation - $75-$150/listing

Open House Signs - Rented and/or installed - $50-$100/listing

Listing Marketing Fee - Listing marketing packages - $300-$600/listing

Individual Property Website - Individual Property website - $50-$100/listing

Listing Presentations - Professional quality printed listing presentation - $25-$50/listing

Just Listed/Just Sold Cards - 100 cards printed/mailed/postage - $100-$200/listing

Listing Photography - Professional listing photography, drone photography - $150-$400/listing

New Agent Training - Typically paid with an increased split - 10-20% additional split

Advanced Training - Annual onsite or offsite training events - $50-$500

Mentoring - Typically paid with an increased split - 10% additional split

Coaching - Coaching fee is split between coach and brokerage $500-$100/month

Other types of models – Base plus commission

One of the most popular brokerages that use this model is Redfin. They pay agents a base salary plus a bonus, as well as expenses and benefits. To see an example of how much an agent can make, they have a helpful tool that lets you select a metro area and see the average compensation and number of transactions.[6]

I include two examples here:

Boston

Transactions
Boston Agents close 19 transactions on average in their first year

Salary + bonuses in first year at Redfin:
$62,000

Expenses covered by Redfin:
$14,000

Benefits paid by Redfin:
$11,000

Total compensation in first year:
$87,000

Total compensation in third year and beyond:
$184,000

Miami

Transactions
Miami Agents close 14 transactions on average in their first year

Salary + bonuses in first year at Redfin:
$49,000

Expenses covered by Redfin:
$14,000

Benefits paid by Redfin:
$11,000

Total compensation in first year:
$74,000

Total compensation in third year and beyond:
$116,000

There is no right or wrong answer when choosing a commission structure. Ultimately it has to be what works best for you and your financial goals and situation. These examples should inform you enough to be able to make an educated decision when discussing with brokerages.

#showmethemoney

CHAPTER 9
Let's go Back to the Future

Many people make a move to real estate after having another career, raising a family, serving in the armed forces, or something else entirely different. There are so many skills that agents have developed in these "previous" careers that can serve them in real estate.

If you were a classroom teacher, there is no doubt you are the master of people management—particularly different personalities and learning styles. You will face these same challenges as a real estate agent. If you can handle an elementary school classroom, there is a good chance you can handle a real estate transaction. Think about the calm demeanor you always needed to keep with your students, because you were the one "in charge". It's only slightly different when working with buyers and sellers on a transaction. You are the one they are looking to for answers, and it's your job to keep things moving and on time.

Did you work in finance? Perfect! You'll be a natural at quickly calculating down payment amounts, monthly HOA fees, and commissions! Numbers play a big role in real estate, and you don't have to be a math whiz, but having a background in numbers or money is definitely an advantage.

Are you a Veteran? The discipline and commitment it took to succeed in the military will serve you well as a real estate agent. Equally important is the camaraderie you will have with other veterans looking to purchase a home and possibly secure a VA loan. This could be a great niche for you to work in.

Stay-at-home moms often think they are the least qualified for this career, but they could not be more wrong. If you can manage a household of screaming children, their schedules, prep meals without burning the house down, and drive to Target while distracted by someone screaming in the back seat, you can handle being a real estate agent. Trust me, it isn't always that different.

It may be helpful to sit down and make a list of skills and strengths that you think you have and then brainstorm ways that those strengths can help you in a real estate career.

Ask yourself: What are some skills that I already have?

Some other good news is that there is no one right way to be a real estate agent. There are as many ways to be successful as there are successful agents. There are some structures and knowledge that help, but in terms of your own career, it's best to leverage the skills you already have.

If you're curious about what kind of skills most real estate agents use, here are 15 of them, borrowed from My VA 360[7].

Communication

You will be talking, texting, and emailing. A lot. With a lot of different people. All with different communication styles. You will need to learn who likes to talk on the phone and who prefers text. Who will bug you all hours of the day and who is super respectful of your time. It's not just the clients you are communicating with. It's other agents, lawyers, title companies, mortgage lenders, and inspectors.

You will be surprised at how many contacts you add

to your phone in your first year of real estate!

Understanding social cues

You know when you're talking to your best friend, and they tell you everything is okay, but you look at them and know it's not? Or when your spouse comes home with a surprise and doesn't want you to know, but it's written all over their face? Those are some social cues. Get used to understanding them. Many times, you'll be showing a home, and without your client saying a word, you can look at their face and know if they love it or hate it.

Integrity and Honesty

This will, hands down, make or break a new agent. If clients learn that you can be trusted, that you've got their back, and that they are safe to ask you anything, they will come back. And they will tell their friends. On the contrary, one small white lie can sink your ship. Be of service to your clients and treat them as you would want to be treated.

Negotiation Skills

As a buyer or seller agent, you represent that person

and have a financial responsibility to them. Your goal is to get them the best and fairest deal possible. A lot of negotiating goes on, often behind the scenes, and it is your job to be the voice of reason and fairness.

Active Listening Skills

Your clients count on you to catch the details and read their emotions. This is where active listening comes in. We are all easily distracted by our phones, but when with your clients, give them your full attention. They need to feel heard.

Problem-solving skills

There will be problems. No matter how organized and thorough you are, things will happen. That's ok. What's more important is how you solve those problems. Sometimes those problems have to do with issues with the property; other times, it's issues with the clients. Be prepared to solve all kinds of problems.

Teaching skills

You're probably thinking, "I'm new at this; how can I possibly teach someone else??" The truth is, as inexperienced as you may be, you still know more than they do. The more you teach, the more you learn yourself, so take advantage of it.

Patience

You will need it. Lots of it. You will be waiting for phone calls to be returned, waiting for the appraisals to come back, and waiting for properties to close. Some things happen quickly, and others take what seems like forever. Just be patient.

Tech-savvy

No one is saying you'll need to build a computer, but make sure you are comfortable navigating websites and using electronic signature software, among other things. There is an entire market of real estate agent-specific technology out there, looking to make our jobs easier, faster, and slicker. Learn what works for you.

Knowledge of the industry

Your first year (or few) in real estate will feel like you are drinking from a fire hose with the amount of information coming at you. Do your best to take it all in. One of the things that can help a newer agent seem less new is knowledge of the industry. Being able to discuss trends in the market, or even in your specific area, is a huge plus when it comes to marketing yourself.

Familiarity with the local area

It's possible you have decided to work in the same area you live, which is great. You already know all the good dog parks, coffee shops, and nearest grocery stores. If you are working in an area outside of where you live, that's cool too. Just make sure to do your best to learn these same things. Clients will want to know about the schools, the public transportation, the restaurants, etc.

Great work ethic

This is not to be confused with burning yourself out. However, being motivated, committed, and hard-working are skills that will help you succeed in this business.

Understanding of architecture

No one expects you to know it all, but being able to tell the difference between a raised ranch and a colonial is one way to make it look like you know what you are talking about. There are plenty of cheat sheets that give an overview of home styles, interior design features, etc. Spend some time learning them.

People skills

This is a tricky one. I always joke that since I'm an introvert, I don't really like people. That is not entirely true. I actually like people, and I have great people skills. No matter where you fall on the introvert/extrovert spectrum, make sure your clients feel like they are your number one priority. Send birthday cards and check in on them.

Time management skills

Unlike any other office job you may have had where your calendar was dictated by meetings and project due dates, as a real estate agent, you are fully responsible for your calendar. This can be challenging because it's possible to always be working or always be sitting on the couch drinking coffee. I've experienced both of these extremes. The hope is that you find someplace in the middle and can balance work and family, making sure you are generating business and money, but also spending time with your family and taking care of yourself.

I know it seems like a lot, but it is totally doable.

#usewhatyougot

CHAPTER 10
How to organize your day

If you previously worked a corporate job, were a teacher, or even a parent, there were things throughout your day that forced you to have an organized and structured schedule. Corporate employee? You had a meeting schedule, check-ins with your boss, and deadlines for deliverables. Classroom teacher? Your life was neatly organized in 45-minute blocks. You had bus duty and lunch duty, not to mention detention and recess. Stay-at-home parent? Your day was ruled by feedings and naptimes, playdates, and dance lessons.

Newsflash, as a real estate agent, you get to make your own schedule. This may sound like a dream come true but let me tell you how quickly it can become a nightmare. Wake up late on Tuesday, lounge around, having a 2nd cup of coffee, then a 3rd. Before you know it, it's noontime and you're still in pajamas. Worse yet, you have not accomplished one single thing. I am telling you this because it has happened to me—more than once. I'm not lazy, but it is easy to take the day (or afternoon) off when you are your own boss. Yes, this is a perk of the job, but be careful not to let it become an everyday thing.

Structuring your day helps you avoid these "on the couch watching reality TV all day" kind of days. It also ensures that you don't overwork yourself to the point of exhaustion. This one I've heard can happen but have never personally experienced. I'm much more in the lazy coffee-drinking category. I have seen agents work long hours day after day without a break, and you may look at them and think, "Wow, they are really working their a$$ off." All those stereotypical "hustle" and "grind" hashtags come to mind. But when was the last time they had dinner with a friend, or read a book just for fun? Or exercised or got a good night's sleep?

Life is about balance, and when you are a real estate agent, it is up to you to create this balance. I am a work in progress but have adopted the time-blocking process to structure my days and ensure that I am getting enough work done, and enough downtime to not get burnt out. I have found that I am good at creating my time block schedule, but less good about actually sticking to it. Like I said, I'm a work in progress. Here is a sample time block schedule.

7:00 AM	**Morning Routine** (exercise, meditation, reading, journaling, etc)
9:00 AM	**Lead Generation Prep** (prepare the list of clients that you plan to call/email/text))
10:00 AM	**Lead Generation** (make those calls, send those emails and texts)
11:00 AM	**Social Media** (strategy, content creation, and posting)
12:00 PM	**Lunch** (alone, with a client, or with family or friends.)
1:00 PM	**Business Servicing** (answer texts, emails, calls, update MLS, any paperwork)
2:00 PM	**Prep for showings** (print MLS sheets, get your GPS set, confirm with agents, etc)
3:00 PM	**Listing Appointments and Client Showings**
6:00 PM	**Personal and Family Time**

Ask yourself: do I like having a scheduled day?

In most states, real estate agents work weekends, but that isn't necessarily a requirement. If you prefer to spend your Saturday or Sunday with family or at church, then by all means, set that boundary and use your time for those things. Just remember that some tasks will need to be shifted to one of the weekdays. As real estate agents, we have the luxury of designing our days in ways that work best for us. I encourage you to consider three things when designing your work schedule (time block or otherwise).

When are you most productive? I am a morning person. Don't ask me to do anything after about 4 pm. I mean, I'll do it, but you won't get the most awake and energetic version of me. Craft your days based on whether you are an early bird, night owl, or something in between. Much of a real estate agent's work takes place mid-morning to early evening. Keep this in mind when arranging your workday. If your clients work "regular" jobs, they won't necessarily be able to see a property at 1 pm, so you will need to plan to meet them at 6 pm when they leave the office.

What are your non-negotiables? If you want to go to every one of your child's soccer games, or don't want to work on Fridays, make that happen. Set those expectations with your clients, have a backup plan or coverage for those times when something absolutely cannot be scheduled any other time, and plan your calendar accordingly. We all want to go above and beyond for our clients, but this doesn't mean sacrificing time with our families or friends. I fully support setting boundaries for yourself and sticking to them. The first few times are hard, but it gets a lot easier once you realize that a good client will respect your commitment to your family, the running club, or your dog.

<u>Build in time for your morning routine, rest, and exercise.</u> If you remember chapter 1, I am a big fan of a morning routine. It doesn't have to happen at 5 am, but it should be a consistent part of your workday. I also fully support rest. Real estate is not for the weary; it is sometimes exhausting, with lots of driving, frustrating phone calls, and demanding clients. Make sure you are giving yourself time to rest. And finally (this advice is for me as much as for you), make time to exercise. You don't want to huff and puff up the stairs when showing a property.

#planyourday

CHAPTER 11
How to "network"

The word "network" literally sends chills down my spine. This is followed closely by nausea. When most people hear this word, they envision a giant room filled with strangers holding business cards. And often, this is exactly what networking is. If you enjoy that medieval torture, go for it. But if you're anything like me, you'd rather get a root canal than make small talk with strangers who may never benefit you or your business.

I am here to tell you that there is another way. In fact, there are many, many other ways. Networking really just means connecting with people who you want to know, build a referral partnership with, or otherwise pass business to. This can be done without sweaty palms and boring business cards.

One of the best ways to do this is by joining a networking group. This is a small group of people (usually between 15-25) who meet regularly to work on their business and learn from each other, while building relationships and referral partners. One of the most widely known of these groups is BNI (Business Networking International). The real estate agent seat is notoriously difficult to get, but it's worth your time if you can land it.

I have found my tribe with the Women's Business League. This networking group also has chapters in different cities and towns; it is limited to women and has similar principles and format to BNI. I founded and co-lead a Women's Business League chapter in Naples, Florida. If you are interested in joining or starting your own chapter, I would love to chat! Schedule time with me here: calendly.com/amyfridhi.

Beyond these organized and official groups, there are myriad opportunities for organic networking. They are all around you if you just take a moment to look.

Do you have a regular coffee shop where you like to grab a latte? Set up shop there once a week with a "real estate" sticker or something on your laptop. Chat with people as they come and go. You'll begin to see the same faces, and they will begin to recognize yours.

Are you a runner? Do you like art? Big fan of reading? Join a group based on an interest of yours and you'll accomplish two things at once. You'll spend some time doing something you love and meet people you already have something in common with! This avoids the usual awkwardness when meeting someone new. You are both in the same group, which means you probably like the same thing, so that's a great conversation starter.

Ask yourself: what are some things I enjoy doing where I can meet people?

One of the things I am most grateful for with my "flexible" schedule is the ability to do more volunteer work. I have previously volunteered at an animal shelter (I scooped litter boxes twice a week at 7 am and loved it) and regularly donate blood and platelets (it's free, the people are friendly, and you usually get snacks). These are all incredible ways to network. Now, I'm not saying the only reason to do them is to find potential business. What I am recommending is that if you like doing things like this anyway, it's a great way to build new relationships.

All the suggestions I've provided so far are in-person. Let's not forget that there is a whole big world wide web that we can also use to network. You can use the good old internet however you want, but I most often use it to build my network of referral partners. One often overlooked revenue stream for real estate agents is referral business. Just because you live in Chicago doesn’t mean you can’t make money on a deal in San Francisco.

By leveraging agent-to-agent partnerships across the country and even the globe, you can confidently refer existing clients, friends, and acquaintances to other agents who work in the city/state/country where the person is moving. In addition to referral agent partnerships in just about every state, I also have partners in Spain, France, the UK, and Turkey, with more on the way!

Be thoughtful about how you build your network. Do it in ways that feel true to you and with people who share your values and work ethic.

#morethanbusinesscards

CHAPTER 12
How to get your clients to love you

The answer is simple, but getting there can be a little more challenging.

Make them feel like they are the only client you have. I remember early in my career, I was working with a first-time homebuyer, and he asked me, "How many clients do you have? You always make me feel like you only work for me." That was an amazing compliment and obviously one I still remember. (If you're reading this, thanks Tom!)

Now let's be honest, you will likely have more than one client at a time, and possibly more than a dozen. It is important to make them feel special and like your attention is only on them. How to do this can be tricky. Choose your words carefully. Never say, "I can't meet you then because I am with other clients." It's ok not to be able to meet them, but no need to make them think they are #2 in line.

Listen. Listen to their comments, about the house, about their dog, and everything else in between. The more they feel listened to, the more they will trust you and like you. As a real estate agent, you may think that the only important details to pay attention to are how many bedrooms and bathrooms they want, and if they are pre-approved for a mortgage.

Not true. Learn about their families and what kind of food they like. You would be surprised how much clients appreciate you knowing about this stuff. More often than not, being aware of what is going on in a client's life can help you with scheduling, understanding their response time, and even why they seem stressed when you meet them after work.

Another fun way this comes into play is with closing gifts. Anyone can buy a bottle of champagne and some flowers. But how about a cruise ship trophy? Yup, true story. I had clients buying their first home, and when we toured the property, the sellers had a cruise ship trophy on display. My buyers commented how their family had one as well, and it was kind of a running joke. Well, I found one on eBay and included it in their closing gift basket.

I've said this before, but one of the easiest ways to get your clients to like you is to be yourself. No one likes hanging out with someone who is fake or inauthentic—

letting your clients see the real you will make them more likely to connect with you.

Your clients want to feel like they can trust you and that you understand and listen to them.

Ask yourself: what makes me feel like someone understands me?

You'll see many agents share pictures of the flashy gifts they give their clients or the elaborate celebrations, and these are all fine and good if that's what works for you. But you don't have to do that. If you are a rural realtor and your clients tend to be less flashy and more modest, meet them where they are. If they love talking about their new livestock or last season's crops, don't forget to ask them about it.

If you are comfortable, follow your clients on social media (this is a fine line that can feel creepy if you aren't yet that close with them). Engaging with their posts will help them feel supported and that you are part of their life. It will also help you to stay connected to them after your transaction is complete and keep you top of mind for future business. Just remember, if they are also following you, you want your posts to represent who you are.

Although I've seen some agents do it, I have a hard rule against one thing: taking time away from the clients I am physically with to take a phone call from another client. There are a few exceptions (and these typically qualify as emergencies), but 99.9% of the time, if I am physically present with a client, whether at a showing, open house, a meeting at the office, or just having coffee, they have my undivided attention.

The goal is to make your client feel like they are your only focus. The reality is that we all (hopefully) have at least a handful of other clients, but they don't need to know that. The greatest compliment you can get is when a client says, "I feel like you only work for me."

Another tip for getting clients to love you is communicating with them in the way that they prefer. When I'm not working, I prefer texting to a phone call. If it's something longer and more detailed, send me an email. I don't really like phone calls; I prefer things in print. This isn't the case for everyone. When meeting a client for the first time, one of the questions I ask is how they prefer their communication.

You'll often find that younger clients prefer text, or even Instagram DM, whereas more mature clients like a good old-fashioned phone call. Regardless of a client's preference, if you need to communicate something that is contractual, legal, or otherwise quite important, please always leave a paper (or digital) trail. You want to be able to reference this, and if it was a phone call, your memory of the details may not be 100%.

Keep in mind, you know your clients best, and you know your personality best. Build authentic connections in ways that feel right for you.

#clientlove

CHAPTER 13
Watch the clock

Are you a night owl or an early bird? There is no wrong answer to this. The only wrong thing is when you call/text someone who is the opposite of what you are. We are not Dolly Parton working 9-to-5, but we also don't need to be insane and contact people all hours of the day. This rule is for your clients as well as other agents. Let me share a little story to illustrate this point.

I am an early bird. It's just the way I work. I don't expect other people to be pouring coffee at 5 am, but I will be. Which means I also don't stay up late. It must be a special occasion if you catch me still awake at 9 pm. So, imagine my surprise when I got a text from an agent at 11 pm on a Saturday. Mind you, we are not besties, nor were we in the middle of a transaction together. This was just an agent who had a question about one of my listings. Fortunately, I had set my phone to do not disturb because sleep is important my friends!

After a few years of never wanting to miss a lead or a call from an agent, which meant being constantly glued to my phone, I realized that I needed to set some boundaries. As they say, you can't put the toothpaste back in the tube, so this was a challenge with existing clients, but I promised myself I would set the expectations up front moving forward.

Ask yourself: Do I know how to put my phone on do not disturb?

When I started interacting with new clients or with an agent on a new transaction, I was careful not to always be available. I don't mean I dodged their calls and waited days to call them back, but I was intentional about when and how I worked. I have a friend who is a rockstar at time blocking her calendar, and when it is "work on social media content" time and a client calls, she doesn't pick up. My jaw hit the floor when I first heard this, but then I realized it's pretty genius.

We are real estate agents. Not heart surgeons or emergency first responders. There are very few things that need our immediate attention or response. Remind yourself of this often. Decide the urgency level that works for you and set those expectations accordingly. The moment your client realizes that you answer their every call in a nanosecond, they will come to expect that, and it will either exhaust you (when you do) or disappoint them (when you don't).

Now, there will be times when you may need to stray from your established boundaries. A competitive offer situation when the listing agent is asking for best and final by 9 pm, a showing appointment that conflicts with your Sunday yoga class but is the only time your clients can see the property before offers are due, etc. You get the picture.

Remember, we are our own boss, so we make our schedule. But if you don't have enough time on task doing things to generate income, your bank account will run dry. Work hard but work smart. If you constantly work 16-hour days, your kids will forget what you look like, and you will burn out before you hit the five-year mark.

Please know that I am not perfect with my time blocking or boundary setting, but I know it's important, and I am a work in progress. I am constantly learning from other agents who seem to have a system that works. The key is that the system works for them. It may need some tweaking to get it to work for me.

I recently came across a post on social media that did a great job of breaking down the 24 hours in a day. We all have the same 24 hours a day as Beyoncé; how you use them matters. Let's assume this basic breakdown:

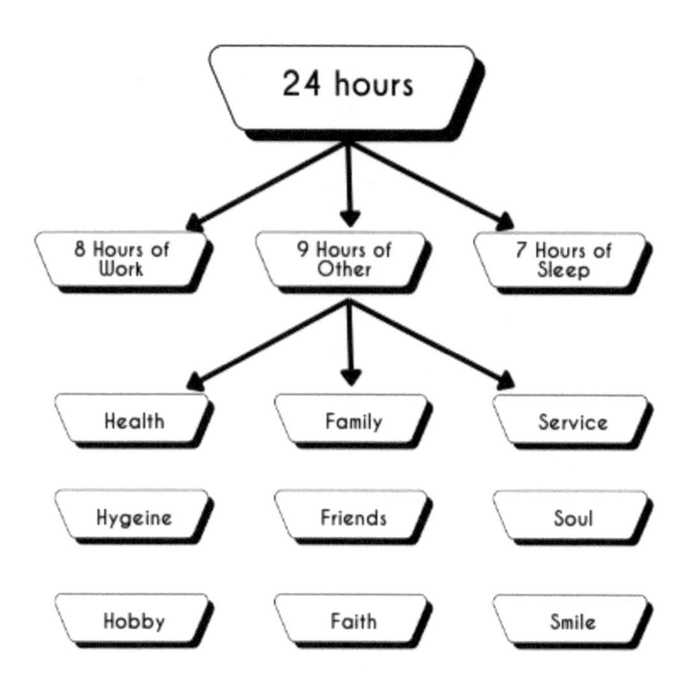

This is just a rough sketch. The bigger picture here is that work is only about a third of your day, and it's important to keep a balance with the rest of the pieces listed here. No one says that the 9 hours allocated to "other" must be divided evenly. Some weeks maybe you spend more time on your hobby than hanging out with friends. Other weeks may be heavy with family commitments and short on service to others (volunteering).

My unsolicited advice is that every day should include health (exercise) and smiling. I am also partial to faith. For me, that's my daily meditation, but for you, it may be prayer, and I make that non-negotiable.

Consider this chart when thinking about how to plan your day and week.

#boundaries

CHAPTER 14
TLDR

So, you didn't want to read the whole thing. I get it. I am the Cliff's Notes generation; if there's a shorter, faster way, I'm here for it too. I still think you should have read all my nuggets of wisdom, but in case you didn't, here is the condensed version.

Your morning routine, more than just coffee

I don't care if you start your day with prayer, yoga, or just a strong cup of coffee, but be consistent. Waking up close to the same time and starting with the same (or similar) routine each day will prepare you for a productive day ahead.

Don't try to be somebody else

What's that Oscar Wilde quote? "Be yourself, everyone else is already taken." It's true. Being your authentic self will make it easier to connect with clients and colleagues. People quickly see through it when you are pretending to be someone or something you are not.

The nuts and bolts of where you work

Unlike searching for a "traditional" job, finding the right real estate brokerage takes some sleuthing and asking the right questions. They will all want you, so the trick is to decide which one you want.

Find your tribe (aka your ideal clients)

There is enough business to go around. If you force yourself to work with clients who aren't a good fit, neither of you will have an awesome experience. Find people you resonate with, and I assure you they will become your biggest cheerleaders.

The alphabet of things

You need to keep toilet paper in your trunk. And an umbrella. And better get familiar with that calculator and laptop.

This isn't Match.com

A large part of your job as a real estate agent is building relationships. With your clients, your colleagues, and even competing agents. Be nice, always. As Benjamin Franklin once said, "You catch more flies with honey than you do with vinegar."

I'm an introvert, how about you?

It's true. People exhaust me. Did you think the title of this book was a joke? Learning your energetic style and how best to use it to your advantage is important.

My money don't jiggle jiggle

We would all be lying if we said we didn't get into real estate for the earning potential. So, make sure you understand your commission structures and who is getting a cut of it.

Let's go back to the future

More than likely, you had a career before real estate. If you didn't, feel free to skip ahead. Whether you were a teacher, an engineer, or a stay-at-home mom, you have skills and talents that you can use in real estate. You just need to identify them.

How to organize your day

As a real estate agent, you are self-employed, which means you make the rules. Want to sleep in? Go for it. You won't get in trouble with your boss, but you also won't make any money. The best bet is to get yourself a schedule and stick to it.

How to "network"

If you love strangers and small talk, by all means, go to as many networking events as you want. But if you're like me and the thought makes you nauseous, find other ways to connect with people to help you grow your business.

How to get your clients to love you

Easy. Be yourself and listen. Seriously, that's it.

Watch the clock

Real estate agents don't work 9 to 5. That doesn't mean you have to work 24/7. Set a schedule and some boundaries to save yourself from getting burned out or forgetting what your kids look like.

#TLDR

Endnotes

[1] https://www.truity.com/test/type-finder-personality-test-new

[2] https://www.truity.com/test/enneagram-personality-test

[3] https://www.researchgate.net/figure/Short-business-portraits-of-the-nine-Enneagram-types_tbl2_253435630

[4] https://www.psychologytoday.com/us/tests/personality/type-personality-test

[5] https://theclose.com/real-estate-broker-agent-commission-split-agreement/

[6] https://www.redfin.com/careers/real-estate/agents

[7] https://myva360.com/blog/15-skills-a-real-estate-agent-must-have

About the Author

Amy Fridhi is a globe-trotting Realtor® and recovering educator. She recently published a chapter in the anthology "Becoming An Unstoppable Woman In Real Estate," which hit best-seller status in seven categories on Amazon.

Amy's decades of experience buying and selling real estate in the US and abroad have helped her grow her business as a coach and mentor for real estate agents. She holds multiple designations and certifications, including Accredited Buyer's Representative (ABR) and Certified Luxury Home Marketing Specialist (CLHMS).

Amy is a licensed Realtor® in multiple states as well as a seasoned investor, is multi-lingual, and a gifted relationship builder. When not searching the MLS, she can be found drinking coffee with her cats on her lanai in sunny Southwest Florida.

Made in the USA
Thornton, CO
08/02/23 16:45:22

8bb89f02-49e2-4743-bae0-632106150dbaR01